EMMANUEL JOSEPH

Choose, Create, Connect, A Guide to Decision-Making, Creativity, and Compassion in Everyday Life

Copyright © 2025 by Emmanuel Joseph

All rights reserved. No part of this publication may be reproduced, stored or transmitted in any form or by any means, electronic, mechanical, photocopying, recording, scanning, or otherwise without written permission from the publisher. It is illegal to copy this book, post it to a website, or distribute it by any other means without permission.

First edition

This book was professionally typeset on Reedsy. Find out more at reedsy.com

Contents

1. Chapter 1: The Power of Choice — 1
2. Chapter 2: The Art of Decision-Making — 3
3. Chapter 3: Embracing Uncertainty — 5
4. Chapter 4: Cultivating Creativity — 6
5. Chapter 5: The Role of Passion — 7
6. Chapter 6: The Magic of Collaboration — 8
7. Chapter 7: Building Empathy — 9
8. Chapter 8: Practicing Compassion — 10
9. Chapter 9: The Joy of Giving — 11
10. Chapter 10: Mindful Living — 12
11. Chapter 11: The Importance of Self-Compassion — 13
12. Chapter 12: Nurturing Relationships — 14
13. Chapter 13: Overcoming Obstacles — 15
14. Chapter 14: Finding Balance — 16
15. Chapter 15: Personal Growth — 17
16. Chapter 16: The Power of Positivity — 18
17. Chapter 17: Living with Purpose — 19

1

Chapter 1: The Power of Choice

Our lives are a series of choices, each one shaping our journey and defining who we are. From the moment we wake up, we are faced with decisions that influence our day, our relationships, and our happiness. The power of choice is immense, and understanding how to harness it can lead to a more fulfilling life.

Every decision, no matter how small, carries weight. The breakfast we choose sets the tone for our morning, while the career path we pursue determines our long-term happiness and success. The ability to make choices is a muscle that strengthens with use and experience. As we navigate through life, each decision we make builds our confidence and shapes our character. By recognizing the power of choice, we can take control of our lives and steer them in the direction we desire.

However, making choices is not always easy. It requires us to balance our intuition with rational thought. While our gut feelings can guide us, it is essential to consider the facts and evaluate the potential outcomes. This chapter explores the various strategies for effective decision-making, from the classic pros and cons list to more sophisticated techniques like the decision matrix and the six thinking hats. By understanding and applying these methods, we can approach decisions with clarity and confidence.

The stories of successful individuals often highlight the importance of decisive action. Consider the story of Steve Jobs, who made bold choices that revolutionized the tech industry. His ability to trust his instincts while also considering the broader picture allowed him to create products that changed the world. By learning from such examples, we can inspire ourselves to make decisions that align with our values and aspirations.

Ultimately, the power of choice lies in our hands. It is up to us to recognize the opportunities before us and make decisions that lead to a more fulfilling and meaningful life. By embracing the power of choice, we can create a future that reflects our true selves and our deepest desires.

2

Chapter 2: The Art of Decision-Making

The art of decision-making is a delicate balance between intuition and rational thought. It requires us to trust our instincts while also considering the facts and potential outcomes. By mastering this art, we can make decisions that align with our values and lead to a more fulfilling life.

One effective strategy for decision-making is the pros and cons list. By listing the advantages and disadvantages of each option, we can gain a clearer understanding of the potential outcomes. This method is simple yet powerful, helping us weigh our choices and make informed decisions.

Another useful technique is the decision matrix, which involves evaluating options based on specific criteria. By assigning scores to each option, we can objectively compare them and identify the best choice. This method is particularly helpful for complex decisions that involve multiple factors.

The six thinking hats technique, developed by Edward de Bono, encourages us to approach decision-making from different perspectives. Each hat represents a different way of thinking, such as logical, emotional, creative, and cautious. By considering the decision from all angles, we can gain a more comprehensive understanding and make better choices.

The art of decision-making is not about eliminating uncertainty but rather about navigating it with confidence and grace. By applying these strategies and trusting our instincts, we can make decisions that lead to a more fulfilling and meaningful life.

3

Chapter 3: Embracing Uncertainty

Uncertainty is an inherent part of life. While it can be uncomfortable, it also presents opportunities for growth and discovery. By embracing uncertainty, we can open ourselves up to new possibilities and experiences.

One way to embrace uncertainty is to reframe it as "productive uncertainty." This concept involves viewing uncertainty as a catalyst for creativity and innovation. When we are uncertain, we are more likely to explore new ideas and solutions. By embracing this mindset, we can turn uncertainty into a powerful tool for personal and professional growth.

Another approach is to practice mindfulness. By staying present in the moment, we can reduce anxiety about the future and focus on what we can control. Mindfulness helps us stay grounded and resilient in the face of uncertainty.

It is also important to develop a growth mindset. By viewing challenges and setbacks as opportunities for learning, we can approach uncertainty with curiosity and optimism. This mindset allows us to thrive in the face of change and uncertainty.

Ultimately, embracing uncertainty is about being open to the unknown and finding strength in the process. By adopting a positive and proactive approach, we can turn uncertainty into a source of inspiration and growth.

4

Chapter 4: Cultivating Creativity

Creativity is a vital skill that enables us to think outside the box, solve problems, and bring new ideas to life. It is not limited to artists and musicians; everyone can cultivate creativity in their daily lives.

One way to nurture creativity is to engage in brainstorming sessions. By allowing ourselves to generate ideas without judgment, we can unlock our creative potential. This process involves suspending our inner critic and embracing a free-flowing mindset.

Creative exercises, such as drawing, writing, or playing music, can also stimulate our imagination. These activities help us tap into our subconscious and explore new possibilities. By setting aside time for creative pursuits, we can keep our creativity alive and thriving.

Collaboration is another powerful tool for fostering creativity. By working with others, we can gain new perspectives and insights. Collaborative projects often lead to richer and more innovative ideas.

Lastly, it is important to create a conducive environment for creativity. Surrounding ourselves with inspiration, whether through art, nature, or stimulating conversations, can fuel our creative spirit. By nurturing our creativity, we can bring more innovation and joy into our lives.

5

Chapter 5: The Role of Passion

Passion is the driving force behind creativity and personal fulfillment. It gives our lives meaning and purpose, fueling our desire to achieve our goals.

To find your passion, it is essential to explore your interests and curiosities. Pay attention to what excites you and brings you joy. By following these sparks of interest, you can uncover your true passions.

Once you have identified your passion, it is important to nurture it. Dedicate time and energy to pursue your interests, even if it means stepping out of your comfort zone. By investing in your passions, you can lead a more fulfilling and joyful life.

Passion also plays a crucial role in overcoming challenges. When we are passionate about something, we are more resilient and motivated to persevere in the face of obstacles. By staying connected to our passions, we can maintain our enthusiasm and drive.

Ultimately, passion is the key to living a meaningful and fulfilling life. By embracing and nurturing our passions, we can create a life that reflects our true selves and our deepest desires.

6

Chapter 6: The Magic of Collaboration

Collaboration brings together diverse perspectives and skills, leading to richer ideas and solutions. It is a powerful tool for achieving our goals and creating meaningful connections with others.

Effective collaboration begins with open communication. By sharing our thoughts, ideas, and concerns, we can build trust and understanding within the group. Active listening is also crucial, as it allows us to truly understand and appreciate the perspectives of others.

Another key aspect of collaboration is recognizing and valuing the strengths of each team member. By leveraging the unique skills and talents of the group, we can achieve more than we could individually. This synergy leads to innovative solutions and successful outcomes.

Collaboration also involves embracing conflict and differences. By addressing disagreements openly and respectfully, we can find common ground and strengthen our relationships. Conflict can be a catalyst for growth and improvement when handled constructively.

Ultimately, the magic of collaboration lies in the collective power of the group. By working together and supporting each other, we can achieve our goals and create lasting, meaningful connections.

7

Chapter 7: Building Empathy

Empathy is the ability to understand and share the feelings of others. It is a crucial component of compassion and connection, allowing us to build stronger, more meaningful relationships.

To build empathy, it is essential to practice active listening. By fully engaging in conversations and focusing on the speaker, we can gain a deeper understanding of their emotions and experiences. This involves suspending judgment and truly listening with an open mind.

Another way to develop empathy is to practice perspective-taking. By putting ourselves in the shoes of others, we can gain insight into their feelings and challenges. This exercise helps us appreciate the unique experiences and viewpoints of those around us.

Empathy also involves expressing compassion and understanding. By acknowledging the emotions of others and offering support, we can create a safe and nurturing environment for our relationships to flourish.

Ultimately, building empathy is about being present and fully engaged in our interactions with others. By developing this skill, we can create stronger connections and foster a more compassionate and understanding world.

Chapter 8: Practicing Compassion

Compassion involves recognizing the suffering of others and taking action to help. It is a powerful force that can transform our lives and the lives of those around us.

To practice compassion, it is important to cultivate a compassionate mindset. This involves being aware of the suffering of others and feeling a genuine desire to help. By developing this mindset, we can become more attuned to the needs of those around us.

Another way to practice compassion is to perform acts of kindness. Whether it is offering a helping hand, listening to someone in need, or simply being there for a friend, small acts of kindness can have a profound impact on others.

Compassion also involves being patient and understanding. By showing empathy and giving others the benefit of the doubt, we can create a more supportive and nurturing environment.

Ultimately, practicing compassion is about making a positive impact on the world. By extending our kindness and understanding to others, we can create a ripple effect of compassion and change.

9

Chapter 9: The Joy of Giving

Giving brings joy not only to the recipient but also to the giver. It is a powerful way to make a positive impact on our communities and enrich our own lives.

One way to experience the joy of giving is through volunteering. By offering our time and skills to help others, we can make a meaningful difference in our communities. Volunteering also provides an opportunity to connect with others and build lasting relationships.

Another way to give back is through random acts of kindness. Simple gestures, such as paying for someone's coffee or offering a compliment, can brighten someone's day and create a sense of connection and happiness.

Giving also involves being generous with our resources. Whether it is donating to a cause we believe in or sharing our possessions with those in need, generosity can have a profound impact on others.

Ultimately, the joy of giving lies in the positive impact we can make on the world. By giving back to our communities and showing kindness to others, we can create a more compassionate and joyful world.

10

Chapter 10: Mindful Living

Mindfulness involves being present in the moment and fully experiencing life as it unfolds. It is a powerful practice that can enhance our overall well-being and happiness.

To practice mindfulness, it is important to cultivate awareness of our thoughts, feelings, and surroundings. This involves paying attention to the present moment without judgment or distraction. By staying present, we can fully experience and appreciate each moment.

Another way to incorporate mindfulness into our daily lives is through meditation. By setting aside time to meditate, we can calm our minds and gain a deeper sense of clarity and focus. Meditation helps us develop a greater awareness of our thoughts and emotions, allowing us to respond to life's challenges with a calm and balanced mind.

Mindfulness also involves practicing gratitude. By taking time to reflect on the positive aspects of our lives, we can cultivate a sense of appreciation and contentment. This practice helps us stay grounded and focused on the present moment.

Ultimately, mindful living is about being fully present and engaged in our lives. By practicing mindfulness, we can reduce stress, increase focus, and enhance our overall well-being.

11

Chapter 11: The Importance of Self-Compassion

Self-compassion involves treating yourself with the same kindness and understanding that you would offer to a friend. It is a crucial component of emotional well-being and personal growth.

To cultivate self-compassion, it is essential to practice self-awareness. By acknowledging our thoughts and feelings without judgment, we can develop a more compassionate and accepting relationship with ourselves. This involves recognizing our imperfections and embracing them as part of our unique journey.

Another way to nurture self-compassion is through positive self-talk. By replacing self-critical thoughts with supportive and encouraging ones, we can boost our self-esteem and foster a healthier self-image. This practice helps us develop a more positive and nurturing inner dialogue.

Self-compassion also involves taking care of our physical and emotional needs. By prioritizing self-care activities, such as exercise, relaxation, and hobbies, we can nurture our overall well-being. This practice helps us recharge and stay resilient in the face of life's challenges.

Ultimately, self-compassion is about being gentle and kind to ourselves. By cultivating this mindset, we can develop a healthier and more positive relationship with ourselves, leading to greater happiness and well-being.

12

Chapter 12: Nurturing Relationships

Healthy relationships are vital to our happiness and well-being. They provide support, companionship, and a sense of belonging. This chapter offers advice on building and maintaining strong, meaningful relationships.

One key aspect of nurturing relationships is effective communication. By openly expressing our thoughts and feelings, we can build trust and understanding with others. Active listening is also crucial, as it allows us to truly understand and appreciate the perspectives of those we care about.

Another important factor is mutual respect. By valuing the opinions, boundaries, and needs of others, we can create a supportive and harmonious environment for our relationships to flourish. This involves showing empathy and compassion in our interactions.

Building strong relationships also requires effort and commitment. By making time for our loved ones and prioritizing our connections, we can strengthen our bonds and create lasting memories. This practice involves being present and fully engaged in our interactions with others.

Ultimately, nurturing relationships is about investing in the people who matter most to us. By building trust, showing respect, and making an effort to connect, we can create strong and meaningful relationships that enrich our lives.

13

Chapter 13: Overcoming Obstacles

Life is full of challenges and obstacles that can hinder our progress. However, these barriers also present opportunities for growth and learning. This chapter provides strategies for overcoming obstacles and achieving your goals.

One effective approach is to develop a growth mindset. By viewing challenges as opportunities for learning and improvement, we can approach obstacles with curiosity and optimism. This mindset helps us stay resilient and motivated in the face of adversity.

Another strategy is to break down larger goals into smaller, manageable steps. By focusing on incremental progress, we can build momentum and maintain our motivation. This approach helps us stay focused and avoid feeling overwhelmed.

It is also important to seek support from others. By reaching out to friends, family, or mentors, we can gain valuable insights and encouragement. This support network can provide the strength and guidance we need to overcome obstacles.

Ultimately, overcoming obstacles is about staying persistent and positive. By adopting a proactive and resilient approach, we can navigate challenges and achieve our goals.

14

Chapter 14: Finding Balance

Balance is essential for a healthy and fulfilling life. It involves finding harmony between various aspects of our lives, such as work, relationships, and self-care. This chapter explores the importance of finding balance and offers practical tips for achieving it.

One way to find balance is to set clear priorities. By identifying what truly matters to us, we can allocate our time and energy accordingly. This involves setting boundaries and making intentional choices about how we spend our time.

Another approach is to practice time management. By organizing our tasks and responsibilities, we can create a more structured and manageable schedule. This practice helps us stay focused and avoid feeling overwhelmed.

Self-care is also a crucial component of balance. By prioritizing activities that nurture our physical and emotional well-being, we can maintain our energy and resilience. This involves making time for relaxation, hobbies, and exercise.

Ultimately, finding balance is about creating harmony in our lives. By setting priorities, managing our time, and prioritizing self-care, we can achieve a healthy and fulfilling life.

15

Chapter 15: Personal Growth

Personal growth is a lifelong journey of self-discovery and improvement. It involves setting goals, embracing change, and continuously striving to become the best version of ourselves.

To foster personal growth, it is important to set clear and achievable goals. By identifying our aspirations and creating a plan to achieve them, we can stay motivated and focused on our journey. This practice helps us measure our progress and celebrate our achievements.

Another key aspect of personal growth is embracing change. By being open to new experiences and challenges, we can expand our horizons and develop new skills. This involves stepping out of our comfort zones and embracing the unknown.

Continuous learning is also crucial for personal growth. By seeking out new knowledge and experiences, we can stay curious and engaged in our journey. This practice helps us stay adaptable and resilient in the face of change.

Ultimately, personal growth is about becoming the best version of ourselves. By setting goals, embracing change, and continuously learning, we can achieve our full potential and lead a fulfilling life.

16

Chapter 16: The Power of Positivity

A positive mindset can transform our life and help us achieve our goals. Positivity enables us to see opportunities where others see obstacles and helps us maintain our motivation and resilience.

To cultivate a positive mindset, it is important to practice gratitude. By taking time each day to reflect on the things we are thankful for, we can shift our focus from what we lack to what we have. This practice helps us develop a more optimistic and appreciative outlook on life.

Another way to foster positivity is to surround ourselves with positive influences. By spending time with supportive and uplifting people, we can create an environment that nurtures our well-being. This involves seeking out relationships and activities that bring us joy and fulfillment.

Positive self-talk is also crucial for maintaining a positive mindset. By replacing negative thoughts with encouraging and supportive ones, we can boost our confidence and resilience. This practice helps us stay focused on our goals and navigate challenges with a positive attitude.

Ultimately, the power of positivity lies in our ability to shift our perspective and focus on the good in every situation. By cultivating a positive mindset, we can create a more fulfilling and joyful life.

17

Chapter 17: Living with Purpose

Living with purpose involves aligning our actions with our values and passions. It is about creating a life that reflects our true selves and makes a positive impact on the world.

To find our purpose, it is important to reflect on our values and passions. By identifying what truly matters to us and what we are passionate about, we can gain clarity on our purpose. This involves exploring our interests, strengths, and aspirations.

Once we have identified our purpose, it is essential to take intentional actions that align with it. By setting goals and creating a plan to achieve them, we can stay focused and motivated on our journey. This practice helps us create a life that is true to ourselves and our values.

Living with purpose also involves making a positive impact on the world. By using our talents and resources to help others, we can create a ripple effect of positive change. This practice helps us find fulfillment and meaning in our lives.

Book Description: "Choose, Create, Connect: A Guide to Decision-Making, Creativity, and Compassion in Everyday Life"

In "Choose, Create, Connect: A Guide to Decision-Making, Creativity, and Compassion in Everyday Life," readers are invited on a journey of self-discovery and empowerment. This engaging guide explores the three pillars of a fulfilling life: decision-making, creativity, and compassion.

Through practical advice, inspiring stories, and actionable strategies, the book empowers readers to harness the power of choice, cultivate their creative potential, and build meaningful connections with others.

The book delves into the art of decision-making, offering techniques and insights to navigate the complexities of life's choices with confidence and clarity. It also explores the importance of creativity, providing tools and exercises to unlock one's creative potential and bring innovation into everyday life. Additionally, the book highlights the significance of compassion, offering guidance on building empathy, practicing kindness, and making a positive impact on the world.

"Choose, Create, Connect" is a comprehensive guide for anyone seeking to lead a more intentional, creative, and compassionate life. Whether you are looking to make better decisions, ignite your creativity, or deepen your connections with others, this book provides the inspiration and practical advice needed to transform your everyday life.

www.ingramcontent.com/pod-product-compliance
Lightning Source LLC
LaVergne TN
LVHW010445070526
838199LV00066B/6212